I0147335

D. F. Sprigg

Short Prayers for Private Use

for every morning and evening of the week

D. F. Sprigg

Short Prayers for Private Use
for every morning and evening of the week

ISBN/EAN: 9783337284961

Printed in Europe, USA, Canada, Australia, Japan

Cover: Foto ©Lupo / pixelio.de

More available books at **www.hansebooks.com**

SHORT P

FO

PRIVATE

FOR

EVERY MORNING
OF THE

SELECTED FROM SOUR

BY

D. F. SPR

NEW

THOMAS W

2 AND 3

To the Rt. Rev. R. H. WILMER, *D.D.*

MY DEAR BISHOP: You asked me more than a year ago to get out a book of short Private Prayers ; but many things prevented. Not long since you renewed the request, saying you felt the need of a short manual of Private Prayers ; that you would like to give a copy to each one of those you confirmed ; that the other volume I had edited, "Aid to Those who Pray in Private," you liked very much, but thought it might be shortened to advantage ; that the ages gone by were times of meditation and introspection, but this was an age of activity which we could not ignore, but must meet wisely and do for it the best we could. I feel the justice of what you say, and so present you with this volume, which, though not a shortened edition of the other book, but a new one, may be what you desire. Should it meet with your approval, I shall feel confident it will be of some help to those who draw nigh to God.

With much affection and respect,

D. F. S.

SUNDAY MORNING.

This is the day the Lord hath made ; may I be joyful and glad therein. This is the day of light ; let my soul, O Lord, be filled with light and peace. *Amen.*

THANKSGIVING.—I yield Thee thanks and praise, O Lord my God, for creating me after thine own image and likeness ; for redeeming me with thy precious blood, and for admitting me into the number of thy children by adoption. I give Thee praise and thanks that Thou didst patiently wait for my amendment from the time of my childhood unto this hour. I glorify and praise Thee for thy often ridding me of troubles and distresses ; for saving me from the punishment of my sins, and for giving me health of body and quietness of soul. For these and all other mercies and benefits of soul and body, asked or unasked, known or unknown, all glory to Thee ; through Jesus Christ our Lord. *Amen.*

CONFESSION. — Almighty and everlasting Father, father of mercies and God of all comfort, I acknowledge that I was born in sin, and that since my birth I have not ceased, nor do cease daily to transgress thy commandments. [Specify such sins as give you trouble.] For these my sins I am sorry. I grieve that I have offended Thee. I do condemn both myself and my sin. But forasmuch as it hath pleased Thee to love me, even when I was thine enemy, and for assurance thereof to give thy only and well-beloved Son, our Lord Jesus Christ, to be a mediator and advocate between Thee and me, promising that I shall obtain whatever I ask in His name, vouchsafe, O most loving God and merciful Father, to pardon and forgive me in His name, and for His sake. And not only to cleanse my heart from all vanity and carelessness and sin, but to guide and govern me by thy Holy Spirit in all my ways, that I may live according to thy holy and heavenly commandments all the days of my life ; through Jesus Christ our Lord. *Amen.*

FOR SPIRITUAL PROGRESS.—O glorious Lord and Saviour, who on the first day of the week didst rise from the dead, and who art the resurrection and the life, I heartily beseech Thee to raise me, by true repentance and lively faith, from the death of sin to the life of righteousness. Make this day a blessing to my soul that I may worship Thee in spirit and in truth ; that I may go to thy house to be joyful and glad in Thee ; that I may listen to my duty with an honest heart in order to practise it ; and grant that the services of this day, both at home and at church, may fit me the more for that rest which remaineth for the people of God ; so that I and they may at length see thy face in peace. *Amen.*

FOR SPIRITUAL JOY.—Almighty God, the redeemer and comforter of mankind, who by thy Holy Spirit hast prepared far greater pleasures than the world knoweth of for such as refuse the false pleasures of the world for thy sake, tempering the troubles of this world with inward and secret solaces, to the intent that, being cheered and refreshed, we should run to Thee with gladder hearts ; grant that the anointing of thy Holy Spirit may cheer my mind with healthful gladness, that I may always serve thee with a joyful heart ; through Jesus Christ our Lord. *Amen.*

FOR OTHERS.—O Lord, I beseech Thee to hearken graciously to the prayers, and accept the praises which are offered unto Thee this day. Bless thy whole church, and that branch especially to which I belong. Grant that all those who confess thy holy name may agree in the truth of thy holy word, and serve Thee to their lives' end. Bless the Bishop and clergy of this diocese, and especially the minister and parish with which I am connected ; that it may grow in peace and love and good works to the praise of thy Name and the salvation of all its members. Grant this and every blessing for all who need ; through Jesus Christ our Lord. *Amen.*

COMMENDATORY.—As I go to thy house this day, O Lord, may I go with a penitent and thankful heart, to the good of my soul and the peace of my spirit. Together with myself, I commend all I love and all thy people ; that we may worship Thee with gladness and serve Thee with sincerity ; through Jesus Christ. *Amen.*

SUNDAY EVENING.

CONFESSION.—O God our heavenly Father, who art gracious and merciful, slow to anger and of great kindness ; have compassion, I beseech Thee, on my sin and weakness. Forgive the coldness of my love, the formality of my worship, and the imperfection of my obedience. Forgive my temper unsubdued and my appetites unchecked. Forgive my often want of truth in word and deed. Forgive my selfishness, my self-indulgence, and my self-will. Forgive my cowardice and slothfulness in thy service. Forgive my affection for the things of this world and my forgetfulness of the things of heaven. Forgive my forgetfulness of our Saviour and His cross. Forgive me, and cleanse my heart by the blood of thy dear Son. that I may go to my rest thy forgiven child ; through the merits and intercession of Jesus Christ our Lord. *Amen.*

FOR CONTRITION. — O Lord God, who despisest not a contrite heart, and forgettest the sins and wickedness of a sinner, in what hour soever he doth mourn and lament his manner of living ; grant unto me true contrition of heart, that I may truly condemn my sinful life past, and be wholly converted unto Thee ; by our Lord and Saviour Jesus Christ. *Amen.*

FOR RENEWAL.—Heavenly Father, renew me in the spirit of my mind, in my thoughts, my words, and life. May old sins pass away and all things be made new in me. May my affections be reclaimed to thy service, that I may love Thee with all my heart, and my neighbor as myself. I have no sufficiency in myself ; my sufficiency is in Thee. Knowing thy will concerning me is my sanctification, may I earnestly and constantly strive to love Thee more and serve Thee better all the days of my life ; through Christ our Lord. *Amen.*

FOR PROTECTION.—When the day is ended, we give ourselves to rest in the night ; so when this life is ended, we rest in death. Vouchsafe therefore, O Lord our defender, to shield me unable to help myself from dangers and temptations. Grant that while my body sleepeth, my soul may rest in Thee. In trust whereof, I will fall asleep and take my rest ; through our Lord and Saviour, Jesus Christ. *Amen.*

FOR FAITH.—Easily, yea too easily, O Lord, do we believe man who is evil and ignorant, but slowly do we believe Thee, who art God, exceeding good and wise. May I from this time believe in Thee, and in thy threats and promises. May thy word be to me all truth, so that I may take it for more certain than the things I see with my eyes or handle with my hands. As faith is thy gift, bestow it upon me, until my eyes see thy salvation, in thy eternal and blessed kingdom ; through Jesus Christ our Lord. *Amen.*

THANKSGIVING.—O God, as thou hast delivered me by the light of thy gospel from the darkness of

error and ignorance, and conveyed me into the kingdom of thy well-beloved Son who gave himself for
my sins, according to thy good pleasure ; for this thy
exceeding love, I thank and praise thy holy name.
And as Thou hast honored me with the copartnership
of the everlasting inheritance of thy dear Son, to be
of that royal priesthood which shall offer the sacrifices
of eternal praise and thanksgiving to thy holy name,
in thy heavenly temple ;—for this thy wonderful goodness, I would take the cup of salvation and call upon
the name of the Lord.   For my health and friends :
for my life and portion ; for all that has made life a
pleasure and not a burden ;—all glory and thanks be
unto Thee, O Father Almighty, world without end.
Amen.

COMMENDATORY.—I commend myself, my soul
and body and possessions ; my family and friends ;
the church and all peoples ; to thy loving care, O
Lord my God.   May I sleep in peace and awake in
safety ; through Jesus Christ our Lord.   *Amen.*

MONDAY MORNING.

THANKSGIVING.—It is a good thing to give thanks unto the Lord, and to sing praises unto thy name, O most Highest ; to tell of thy loving kindness early in the morning and of thy truth in the night season. Many and great have been the favors and mercies Thou hast bestowed upon me, for which I bless and praise thy holy name. I thank Thee for the blessings of the past night. I thank Thee that I was born of honest and religious parents and in a Christian country. I thank Thee that I was early introduced into the Christian church. I thank Thee that I was permitted on yesterday to worship Thee in the great congregation. And for all the known, and for all the unobserved favors, deliverances, and opportunities of getting and doing good vouchsafed to me and those I love, I bless thy holy providence, and beseech Thee to accept my thanks and make me more thankful ; through Jesus Christ our Lord. *Amen.*

CONFESSION.—" The publican standing afar off, would not so much as lift up his eyes to heaven ; but smote upon his breast, saying, God, be merciful to me a sinner." So, O Lord God, have mercy upon me who have sinned in thought, in word, and deed. [Confess the sins your conscience accuses you of.] O Lord, I know not all my sins, nor the wickedness of

them ; they are more in number than the hairs of my
head.   But O blessed Advocate, who art able to save
forever them who come unto Thee, seeing Thou ever
livest to make intercession for us, I put myself and
my cause into thy hands ; let thy grace forgive me ;
thy power defend me ; thy blood and merits plead for
me and supply all the defects of my confession and
repentance, and procure for me full pardon and grace
to live this day a truthful, honest, and godly life,
that I may find mercy at the great day. *Amen.*

FOR GOD'S BLESSING.—O God, who hast taught us
to cast all our care on Thee, because Thou carest for
us, bless, I beseech Thee, my labor, my occupation,
my friends and relatives, my worldly goods and possessions, that, being free from all undue care and
anxiety concerning this present life, and setting my
affections on things above, I may this day serve Thee
cheerfully and help my neighbors readily to thy honor
and glory ; for the love of Jesus Christ, thy Son, our
Lord. *Amen.*

FOR STRENGTH.—O Lord, who hast told us to
watch and pray that we enter not into temptation,
give me, I beseech Thee, such strong desire to please
Thee, that knowing the weakness of my mortal nature, I may flee with all my might from everything
which may tempt me to offend against Thee, our
loving father ; this I beg for the sake of thy dear Son,
Jesus Christ our Lord. *Amen.*

FOR RULERS.—O God, whose kingdom ruleth over

all, I pray for thy blessing on all who have authority in Church or State ; that by their wise and good administration of the laws, and our careful obedience to the same, I and all people may lead a quiet and peaceable life in all godliness and honesty ; through thy Son, our Lord. *Amen.*

COMMENDATORY.—I commend myself this day to Almighty God, my heavenly Father ; that I may be kept from all sin and danger ; through Jesus Christ. *Amen.*

MONDAY EVENING.

CONFESSION.—At the close of this day, O Heavenly Father, I confess my sins, my imperfections, and infirmities. I have sinned in thought, in speech, in act. [Specify them.] I am not worthy to be called thy son. If, Thou, Lord, shouldst be extreme to mark what I have done amiss, I could not abide it. But have mercy upon me according to thy loving kindness. Cast me not away from thy presence. Take not thy Holy Spirit from me ; but grant that by His holy inspiration I may think and speak those things that are good, and by thy grace perform the same this day and all the days of my life ; through Jesus Christ. *Amen.*

FOR OBEDIENCE.—Almighty God, teach me to submit to the easy yoke of our Saviour, Christ, and to take upon me His light burden. Incline me unto all holy obedience to thy will. May my heart be so rooted and grounded in love, that no difficulties may discourage me in the way of well doing ; and that neither the cares nor pleasures of life may lead me astray from Thee. Increase in me that which is lacking ; raise up in me that which is fallen ; restore to me that which I have lost ; quicken in me that which may be ready to die ; so that I may serve and obey Thee in all things ; through Jesus Christ our Lord. *Amen.*

FOR PURITY.—Blessed Lord, who hast redeemed us unto God by thy blood and hast consecrated all thy people to be temples of the Holy Spirit ; make me a fit dwelling place for thy Spirit. Cast out of me every thing that defileth ; all impure lusts, sinful affections, covetous desires, vain imaginations, and everything contrary to thy holy will, that I may serve Thee this day with a pure and humble mind ; through Jesus Christ our Lord. *Amen.*

FOR MEEKNESS.—O Lord Jesus, who when Thou wast reviled didst not revile again ; when Thou sufferedst didst not threaten, but didst commit thyself to Him who judgeth righteously ; give me the like spirit of meekness and patience, that I may repress all wrath, strife, murmuring, malice, and envy ; that I may refrain from all peevish dispositions and from that unevenness of spirit which hinders me from the discharge of my duty and from giving pleasure to those around me ; I ask these blessings through Jesus Christ. *Amen.*

THANKSGIVING. — Almighty God and Heavenly Father. who of thy gracious providence and tender mercy hast preserved me, I humbly praise and magnify thy glorious name for all thy goodness to me this day. If I have walked uprightly and honestly and truthfully ; if I have kept my tongue as with a bridle, it is of thy mercy, O Lord, my God ; therefore thanks and praise be to Thee this night ; through Jesus Christ. *Amen.*

FOR OTHERS.—O Lord, I pray for the church, that it may grow like Christ ; for the world, that it may be turned to Thee ; for my native land, that it may be governed after thy will ; for my family, my kinsmen according to the flesh, my friends and enemies if I have any ; that all may partake of thy grace here and of glory hereafter ; through our Lord and Saviour Jesus Christ. *Amen.*

COMMENDATORY.—I commend myself, my soul, my body, my possessions, my good name, all I have, all I hope for, all I fear, to my Lord and Saviour, Jesus Christ. *Amen.*

TUESDAY MORNING.

THANKSGIVING.—Almighty God, who savest our life from destruction, and crownest us with mercy and loving kindness, I give Thee heartfelt thanks that Thou hast brought me in peace and safety to see the light of another day. For this and for all thy mercies by day and by night, in sorrow and in gladness, in health and in sickness, at home and abroad, in rest and in journeyings, I praise Thee and will give Thee praise. Above all, for the mercies of pardon and peace through Jesus Christ, I yield Thee unfeigned thanks, O Lord, my God. *Amen.*

FOR RIGHT LIVING.—Grant, O heavenly Father, that I may live this day as thy child. Give me resolution to deny all sinful inclinations ; to subdue all corrupt affections ; to take revenge for my intemperance by mortification ; for mis-spending my time by retirement ; for the errors of my tongue by silence ; for all the sins of my life by deep humility and repentance. And while penitent for my sins, may I be joyful and glad in Thee, so that by the brightness of my life and the cheerfulness of my conversation, I may commend the religion and church of Christ to all I converse with ; through Jesus Christ, our Lord. *Amen.*

FOR LOVE.—O holy and gracious God, who art

infinitely excellent in thyself, and infinitely lovely and bountiful to the sons of men, suffer not my heart to be so hardened by worldly desires, as to resist thy exceeding love and goodness. Take this unworthy heart of mine as thine own ; refine it with the purifying fire of thy love ; give me such fervent, perfect, and sincere love of Thee, as may cast all fear and sloth out of my heart, so that nothing may seem too hard to bear, or too difficult to do for thy sake, through Jesus Christ, our Lord. *Amen.*

FOR PARDON.—Grant unto me, O heavenly Father, perfect remission and forgiveness for all the sins and wickedness, all the errors, the follies, the ignorances, the negligences, the vain thoughts, the rash words, and the many acts of which I have been guilty. And vouchsafe unto me the communion of the Holy Spirit, to be with me as a spirit of sanctification to purify my heart, a spirit of counsel in all perplexities, of direction in all doubts, of resolution in all dangers, of constancy in all trials, and of comfort in all sufferings. Uphold me in those things I have learned aright, and set me right in those things in which I err. Strengthen me if in any good thing I waver, and keep me from all things that may hurt me ; through Christ our Lord. *Amen.*

INTERCESSION.—I call to mind this day, O Lord, before Thee, all who are near and dear to me ; beseeching Thee to remember them for good, and to supply their desires and wants as may be most expedient for them. To those in sickness or sorrow, grant relief ; to those tempted, bestow deliverance ; to those careless, give repentance ; to those in doubt, give assurance. And with all honesty of desire, I commend to thy mercy all who have wronged me by word or deed, beseeching Thee to forgive them all their sins, and to bring them with me to thy heavenly kingdom ; through Christ our Lord. *Amen.*

COMMENDATORY.—Into thy loving hands. and into thy mighty grace, O God, I solemnly commend my soul and body ; that my soul may be kept from sin, and my body from danger ; to serve Thee with a happy spirit and a contented mind ; through our Lord and Saviour, Jesus Christ. *Amen.*

TUESDAY EVENING.

CONFESSION.—O Lord, my God, I confess this night the sins of my childhood, the sins of my youth, and the sins of my riper age ; the sins of my soul and the sins of my body ; my secret sins and my presumptuous sins ; the sins I have done to please myself and the sins I have done to please others. I confess my idle and my reckless sins ; my serious and deliberate sins ; the sins I have striven to hide from others that now I have hid them from my own memory. [Confess those of which you have been guilty to-day.] O Lord, my God, make my confession honest and sincere ; through Jesus Christ our Lord. *Amen.*

FOR PARDON.—O merciful Lord and God, I have sinned, but I do not hide my sins, for I have confessed them before Thee. Forgive them not for my own merits or goodness, but for the merits and worthiness of our Lord Jesus Christ, who died the just for the unjust, that He might bring us unto Thee. For the sake of His atonement upon the cross, may all my sins be blotted out, so that I may serve Thee acceptably, and at last attain eternal life with Thee ; and to Thee shall be all the praise now and forever. *Amen.*

FOR THE HOLY SPIRIT.—O blessed Lord, who hast promised to give Thy Holy Spirit to them that ask

Thee, and art more willing to bestow this gift than I to ask for it, give me the increase of thy heavenly Spirit, that He may bear witness with my spirit that I am thy child and heir of thy kingdom ; and that by the operation of His grace, I may kill all my carnal lusts and evil affections contrary to thy will ; , for the worthiness of thy Son. *Amen.*

FOR RIGHT LIVING.—Almighty God, who knowest I am weak and tempted and easily led into sin, help me to walk uprightly and in thy fear all the days of my life. Make me pure in thought ; truthful and kind in speech ; honest and upright in my dealings with my fellow-men. Give me humility that I be not vain ; patience that I be not angry; kindness to others that I be not selfish. May I always live so as never to be afraid or unprepared to die ; all this, through Jesus Christ our Lord. *Amen.*

FOR PERSEVERANCE.—Give me grace, O Lord, to lay aside every weight and the sin which doth so easily beset me, to run with patience the race that is set before me, looking unto Jesus, the author and finisher of our faith, who for the joy that was set before Him, endured the cross, despising the shame, and is set down at the right hand of the throne of God. *Amen.*

FOR OTHERS.—Heavenly Father, as Thou hast taught us in thy holy word to make intercession, I beseech Thee of thy tender love, to bless my—[specify wife, husband, parents, children, brothers, sisters,

255

friends, etc.] Thou knowest what they need, supply them ; how they have sinned, forgive them ; their
temptations, succor them ; their sorrows, comfort
them ; keep them from all evil and make them to
continue in thy love and service to their life's end ;
and after the course of the world is ended, bring us
all to thine everlasting kingdom ; through Jesus
Christ our Lord. *Amen.*

COMMENDATORY.—

> Lord, keep me safe this night,
>   Secure from all my fears ;
> May angels guard me while I sleep,
>   Till morning light appears.   *Amen.*

WEDNESDAY MORNING.

THANKSGIVING.—Goodness and mercy have fol-lowed me all the days of my life ; may I dwell with God forever ! I acknowledge, Heavenly Father, thy great and undeserved goodness in guarding me and those I love, through the night past ; guard us until we come to thy everlasting kingdom. I thank Thee for all thy mercies the least of which I am not worthy. I thank Thee for sleep, for health, for food, for raiment, for home, for reason, for affections, for friends, for a quiet spirit, for grace and all the means of grace, for the Bible and prayer, for the church with its ministries of truth and love, and for all the bless-ings which have made me and keep me thine. All praise to Thee, O Lord my God ; through Jesus Christ our Lord. *Amen.*

FOR GRACE.—O Lord God, remove from me all iniquity, superstition, and hypocrisy ; all haughtiness, strife, and wrath ; all indolence and fraud ; all lying and injuriousness ; every evil notion, impure thought, and base desire. Grant me to be truly religious and godly ; give me patience and a good temper ; purity and soberness ; contentment and truth, with perse-verance in all good to the end ; through Jesus Christ. *Amen.*

PROFESSION OF FAITH.—I believe in Thee, O Father Almighty. Behold then, as Thou art my

Father and I thy son, as a father pitieth, so be Thou
of tender mercy to me, O Lord.   I believe in Jesus
Christ, and that He came into the world to save sinners.   Thou who camest to save sinners, save Thou
me.   Thou who camest to save the lost, never suffer,
O Lord, that to be lost which Thou hast saved.   I
believe that the Holy Spirit is the Lord and giver of
life.   Thou who gavest me a living soul, give me
that I receive not my soul in vain.   I believe that the
Spirit gives grace, give me that I receive not His
grace in vain.   Our fathers hoped in Thee, they
trusted in Thee and Thou didst deliver them ; they
put their trust in Thee and were not confounded.   O
Lord, in Thee have I put my trust ; let me never be
confounded.   *Amen.*

For Mercy.— Have mercy upon me, O God, after
thy great goodness ; according to the multitude of
thy mercies do away mine offences.   Wash me
thoroughly from my wickedness and cleanse me from
my sin.   I acknowledge my faults and my sins are
ever before me.   Against Thee only have I sinned
and done evil in thy sight.   Thou shalt purge me
with hyssop, and I shall be clean ; Thou shalt wash
me, and I shall be whiter than snow.   Thou shalt
make me hear of joy and gladness, that the bones
which Thou hast broken may rejoice.   Turn thy face
away from my sins, and put out all my misdeeds.
Make me a clean heart, O God, and renew a right
spirit within me.   Cast me not away from thy presence, and take not thy Holy Spirit from me.   *Amen.*

COMMENDATORY.—As I go forth to the duties of this day, remembering the snares and trials and temptations which await me, I commend myself to Thee, O Lord, humbly asking that thy grace may help me, thy mercy defend me, and thy good Spirit aid me, so that I may not yield to sin ; for the glory of thy name, through Jesus Christ our Lord. *Amen.*

WEDNESDAY EVENING.

CONFESSION.—O Lord God, I would make humble and honest confession of my sins to Thee this night. Thou hast comforted us by saying, if we confess our sins, Thou art faithful and righteous to forgive them. I know that though I have confessed Thee with my tongue, I have oftentimes denied Thee by my acts. My eyes have been often opened to let in sin ; my ears have been often ready to receive sinful discourse ; I have let loose my tongue ; I have yielded my members as instruments of sin ; I have defiled my heart by vain and foolish and impure imaginations ; I have wasted my time and have not lived answerably to my means of grace. If Thou, Lord, shouldst be extreme to mark what I have done amiss, I should have no hope. But there is mercy with Thee ; let thy mercy rest upon me now, henceforth and forever ; for Jesus Christ's sake. *Amen.*

FOR TRUST.—Almighty God, who never failest them who put their trust in Thee, help me to put all my trust in Thee and Thee alone. In all my difficulties may I have recourse to Thee ; in all troubles to rest and depend upon Thee. Thou wilt keep him in perfect peace whose mind is stayed on Thee ; let me stay myself upon Thee, that Thou who art the confidence of all the ends of the earth, may be my confidence forever. I would commit myself to the ordering of thy providence, so as to be careful for nothing, but always to be of the number of thy faithful children. Grant me this abiding trust; through Christ our Lord. *Amen.*

FOR FAITH.—Without faith it is impossible to please God ; therefore, O Lord, give me faith which worketh by love and shows itself by holy living. This is the victory that overcometh the world ; give me faith so that I may overcome the temptations of the world, the flesh and the devil, and to be made wholly conformed to the image of Christ in whom I believe ; that at the last I may receive the end of my faith, even the salvation of my soul. Lord, I believe ; help Thou mine unbelief. *Amen.*

FOR PROTECTION.—O God, whose never failing providence ordereth all things both in heaven and earth, I humbly beseech Thee to put away from me all hurtful things and to give me those things which are profitable for me ; through Jesus Christ our Lord. *Amen.*

THANKSGIVING.—Most gracious God, thy tender mercy is over all thy works, and hath in an especial manner been over me. Make me truly sensible of all thy mercy, and give me a heart ever filled with gratitude ; a mouth ever ready to express my thankfulness ; and a life ever ready to show it forth by keeping thy commandments ; through Christ our Lord. *Amen.*

COMMENDATORY.—To God the Father, Son, and Holy Ghost, I commend my soul and body, my family and friends. Grant me quiet and refreshing sleep. Put far from me all wordly cares and earthly fears. Give me holy and loving thoughts of Thee. May I repose in peace with Thee and in love to all mankind. *Amen.*

THURSDAY MORNING.

THANKSGIVING.—"The mountains shall depart, and the hills be removed, but my kindness shall not depart from Thee, neither shall the covenant of my peace be removed, saith the Lord that hath mercy on Thee." So, O Lord, do I believe and I thank Thee. I thank Thee for precious promises and for prevailing grace ; for my nurture and guidance ; for my call and recall; for thy forbearance and long suffering; for all the good received and the success granted me; for the use of things present and the hope of good things to come. What reward shall I give unto the Lord for all the benefits He hath done unto me ? What thanks can I recompense unto God for all He hath spared and borne with me until now ? Holy, holy, holy, Lord God Almighty, I give Thee thanks ; through Jesus Christ our Lord. *Amen.*

FOR RIGHT LIVING.—O Lord God, as I go forth to my duty and labor until the evening, give me patience under trials, kind speech under provocation, truthful words under temptations, fair and honorable dealing toward all mankind. May I bear no malice or hatred in my heart. May I keep my body in temperance, soberness, and chastity. May I not covet or desire other men's goods, but learn and labor truly to get mine own living and to do my duty in that state of life in which Thou hast called me ; through Christ our Lord. *Amen.*

FOR GRACE.—O Lord Jesus Christ, who art made unto us of God, wisdom by revealing Him and His glorious perfection ; righteousness by satisfying the justice of God in our nature ; sanctification by procuring for us the Holy Ghost, and restoring us to God's favor ; redemption by redeeming us from death eternal ; be wisdom and righteousness and sanctification and redemption unto me, now and forever. *Amen.*

FOR THE SPIRIT.—O God, who as on this day didst exalt thy blessed Son with thy right hand to be a prince and a Saviour, leave me not comfortless, but give me the spirit of adoption whereby I may cry Abba, Father, and apply to Thee through Jesus Christ, not as to an angry judge, but as to a merciful and loving Father, so that I may serve Thee joyfully and love Thee fervently. *Amen.*

FOR OTHERS.—Bless, O Lord, those whom Thou hast set over me both in Church and State : govern their hearts in thy fear, and guide their understandings to do those things acceptable to Thee and beneficial to the Church and Commonwealth. Comfort the helpless, and show the light of thy truth to those who wander from the right way. Give to all sinners true repentance. Strengthen those who have begun well, that they may persevere in goodness ; and to all my kindred, friends, and enemies (if I have any) give thy good blessings ; and may the time soon come when all ends of the earth shall see the salvation of God; I ask all, through Jesus Christ our Lord. *Amen.*

COMMENDATORY.—Spared to see another day in health and peace, before going forth to my appointed work, I commend myself to the God and Father of our Lord Jesus Christ ; beseeching Him to keep me from all sin and danger, that I may live as in His presence and be joyful and glad in Him all this day. *Amen.*

THURSDAY EVENING.

CONFESSION.—O Lord, our heavenly Father, merciful and gracious, long suffering and abundant in goodness and truth ; I call to mind thy exceeding love in having redeemed me with the precious blood of Christ, lest the consciousness of my sins should drive me to despair. I know I have sinned in thought, in word, in deed. [Make particular mention of your sins.] Lord make me truly penitent, that I may abhor myself for the sins I have committed, and turn unto Thee with full purpose to lead a sober, righteous, and godly life ; through Jesus Christ. *Amen.*

FOR GRACE.—Almighty God, may thy Holy Spirit in all things direct and rule my heart. Increase my faith, and enlarge my sense of thy love. May my thoughts be continually replenished and contented with a steadfast hope of the good things Thou hast prepared for them who love Thee. May the blessed hope of everlasting life lodge always in the secret of my heart, to be unto me a defence against the cares of this world, the deceitfulness of riches, and the allurements of vain things which cannot help or profit. And grant that, as I advance step by step toward the end of my pilgrimage, I may become more meet for heaven ; through the merits and satisfaction of Jesus Christ our Lord and Saviour. *Amen.*

THANKSGIVING.—Our Father which art in heaven, the giver of all good and the source of all blessedness, I draw nigh to thank Thee for thy manifold gifts and favors, and for the supply of everything I have needed. I thank Thee for the health and strength by which I have been able to perform my duties ; for kind friends who have cheered me ; for a quiet mind that has enlivened me ; for all the good of this life and the expectation of good to come. Accept my thanks, and make me more grateful to Thee for thy abundant blessings ; through Jesus Christ our Lord. *Amen.*

FOR BLESSINGS.—Heavenly Father, teach me to accommodate myself to my condition, that I be not envious of those who possess abundance greater than my own. So far as it shall be thy will to enlarge my portion of this world's goods, suffer me not to set my affections upon them, but may my treasure be ever in Thee. Free my heart from envy, jealousy, covetousness, pride, anger, impatience, and all sin. Give me kindness, gentleness, purity, truth, integrity, and every virtue ; and daily may I grow in grace and in the knowledge of our Lord and Saviour Jesus Christ. *Amen.*

FOR OTHERS.—O Lord, Thou knowest the wants of all I love, supply them ; and in so doing bestow thy blessing which maketh rich. Be gracious to thy Church, that it may grow in goodness, and with its branches cover the earth. Bless all in authority that they may punish wickedness and maintain virtue. Give repentance to all sinners and holiness to all nations ; through Jesus Christ. *Amen.*

COMMENDATORY.—As I lie down this night, O Lord, 1 would lie down in the faith of Christ, in the love of God, and in charity with the world. Prepare me for the time I shall lie down in the grave ; through Him who is the resurrection and the life. *Amen.*

FRIDAY MORNING.

THANKSGIVING.—O God of goodness, who on man's transgressing didst not pass him by nor leave him helpless, but gave him promise of salvation, and in the fulness of time didst send thy Son to take on Him our nature, and by His obedience unto death, didst take away the curse of the law, and by His death didst redeem me and all mankind : Blessed be thy name, and praised and magnified be its record and every memorial of it. Worthy is the Lamb that was slain, as on this day of the week, to receive power and riches and wisdom and strength and honor and glory and blessing. To Him that sitteth upon the throne and to the Lamb, be the blessing and the thanks and the honor and the glory and the might : for ever and ever. *Amen.*

LITANY OF REDEMPTION.—O Lord Jesus Christ, who didst on this day redeem me by thy precious death, that Thou mightest renew in me the image of Him that created me ; *Have mercy upon me.*

By thy exceeding sorrow of soul even unto death, by the prayer three times repeated, by the bloody sweat ; *Have mercy upon me, O Lord.*

By thy bearing of the cross, by the nailing of thy hands and feet, by the burning thirst, by the great and bitter cry : *Have mercy upon me, O Lord.*

By the finishing of thy blessed work, by the commending of thy soul to God, by thy precious death ; *Have mercy upon me, O Lord.*

That I may never forget the pains and sorrows by which Thou didst redeem me ; that I may never forget the exceeding love which endured the cross for my sake ; *Hear me, I beseech Thee.*

That I may never forget the hateful evil of the sin which required my redemption ; that my body of sin may be crucified with Thee. that henceforth I may serve sin no more ; *Hear me, I beseech Thee.*

O most loving Christ, may I love Thee as Thou dost so love me.   And may the God of peace sanctify me wholly ; and may my whole spirit and soul and body be preserved blameless unto the coming of our Lord Jesus Christ. *Amen.*

FOR OTHERS.—O eternal God, the Father of all mankind, have mercy on the whole human race. Pity their ignorance, their foolishness, their weakness, their sin. Sheep wandering on the mountain without a shepherd, travellers lost in the wilderness without a guide. Set up an ensign for the nations and bring them to thy glorious rest.   Hasten thy kingdom, and bring in everlasting righteousness, for the honor of thy Son, who died the just for the unjust, that He might bring them unto God. *Amen.*

FOR HOPE.—Almighty father, who hast prepared everlasting life for all thy people. grant unto me a sure hope of that life everlasting. that I, so long as I live here below, may have some foretaste of it in my heart ; through the merits and deserving of Him, who this day died for me, thy Son, Jesus Christ. *Amen*.

FOR A BLESSING.—O Lord, I am thine, and all that I have is thy gift. Instruct me both to be full and to be hungry, to abound and to suffer need, and in whatsoever state I am, therewith to be content. Make me grateful and liberal in prosperity ; patient and cheerful in adversity ; for the love of Jesus Christ, our Lord. *Amen*.

COMMENDATORY.—As I go out this day, O Lord, not knowing what the day may bring forth, I commit myself to thy care and keeping. The Lord bless me and keep me. The Lord make His face to shine upon me and be gracious unto me. The Lord lift up the light of His countenance upon me and give me peace now and through the day. *Amen*.

FRIDAY EVENING.

CONFESSION.—Lord, sanctify and forgive any that I have tempted to evil by my words and example ; instruct those in the right way whom I may have led into error, and let me never run further in the ways of sin.   Blot out all the evils I have done or tempted others to do, by the power of Thy passion and the blood of Thy cross.   Give me a deep and exceeding repentance, a free and gracious pardon, that Thou mayest answer for me, and enable me to stand upright in judgment ; for in Thee, O Lord, do I put my trust.   Pity me and instruct me ; guide me and support me ; pardon me and save me, for Thy mercy's sake, O loving Saviour.   *Amen.*

FOR PARDON AND SANCTIFICATION. — O Thou, whose hands for my sake were pierced with sharp nails ! whatsoever evil I have by my hands committed, whatsoever good I have left unwrought ; forgive me, Good Lord.

O Thou, whose feet for my sake were fastened to the cross ! whereinsoever my feet have been swift to do evil, or have been slow on errands of love and mercy ; forgive me, Good Lord.

O Thou, whose side for my sake was pierced with a spear ! in whatsoever. my mind has been vain and foolish, and my heart evil and corrupt ; forgive me, Good Lord.

O Thou, who didst bear my sins in Thine own body on the tree, forgive me that I have yielded my body an instrument of unrighteousness unto sin ; and give me grace to present it a living sacrifice, holy, acceptable unto God, which is my reasonable service.

O Thou, who didst bear holy and bitter sufferings for me throughout this day, grant that what Thou wast content to endure for me and my salvation, may be effectual for the saving of my soul.

O Thou, who didst vouchsafe to taste death for every man! mortify in me all things contrary to Thy holy will ; that I may be crucified to the world and alive to Thee. *Amen.*

AGAINST SPIRITUAL SLOTH.—O God, our heavenly Father, give me such a measure of Thy grace that, forgetting those things which are behind, and reaching forth unto those things which are before, I may press toward the mark for the prize of the high calling of God in Christ Jesus ; to whom, with Thee and the Holy Ghost, be honor and glory, world without end. *Amen.*

FOR THE CHURCH.—Almighty Father, of whom the whole family in heaven and earth is named, mercifully look upon the same. Raise up unto the Church on earth men full of faith and of the Holy Ghost, mighty in the Scriptures, able ministers of the New Testament, to go forth with glad heart and ready mind to preach the Gospel to all the nations. Be with them, and so bless them in their work, that Thy word may have free course and be glorified, the fulness of the Gentiles come in, and all Israel be saved ; and we with them, being built upon the foundation of the Apostles and Prophets, Jesus Christ himself being the chief corner-stone, may grow together into an holy temple in the Lord, who livest and reignest with Thee and the Holy Ghost, world without end. *Amen.*

THANKSGIVING.—For all God's mercies of creation and protection, for all Christ's mercies of redemption and salvation, for all the Holy Spirit's mercies of regeneration and sanctification, I render praise and thanksgiving, praying that I may persevere with increased thankfulness to my life's end. *Amen.*

SATURDAY MORNING.

THANKSGIVING. — Accept, O merciful Father, my morning sacrifice of praise and thanksgiving for all the blessings of the night and the mercies of the week. To Thee I owe all I am and all I have. Thou hast not dealt with me after my sins, nor rewarded me according to my iniquities. May the appreciation of thy goodness so grow on me, that I may love Thee more and serve Thee better; through Christ our Lord. *Amen.*

FOR HOLY LIVING.—Almighty God, as Thou hast promised to give Thy Holy Spirit to them that ask Thee, I humbly pray for this gift, that I may be kept from carelessness of spirit and hardness of heart; from fretfulness and impatience; from vanity and pride; from irreverence and indevotion; from repining at thy dispensations and neglecting thy warnings; and from all sin and wickedness. Give to me such love and joy and peace and long-suffering and gentleness and goodness and faith and meekness and temperance, that I may daily crucify the flesh, with its affections and lusts. And this I beg for Jesus Christ's sake. *Amen.*

FOR WATCHFULNESS.—O Lord Jesus Christ, who, in leaving thy Household the Church, didst give to every man his work and hast commanded us to watch, make me diligent in doing the work Thou hast appointed for me ; and always to be patient in hoping and watching for thine Advent, when Thou shalt so come in like manner as thy disciples saw Thee go into heaven. *Amen.*

FOR OUR NEIGHBORS.—Soften my heart, O Lord, that I may be moved at the necessities and griefs of others. O most mild and merciful Christ, I beseech Thee, breathe upon me the Spirit of thy meekness and goodness ; that like as thy pity made Thee to endure most bitter death for us, so my pitying of them may lead me to succor all those who need it, and to the uttermost of my power. *Amen.*

FOR KNOWLEDGE.—Lord Jesus, who art a living fountain to them that know Thee, perpetual food to them that hunger after Thee, glory to them that seek Thee, joy to them that find Thee ; may I seek and find and know Thee, as the one only and everlasting good, in whom are pardon and peace and everlasting felicity now and for ever. *Amen.*

FOR PATIENCE.—Almighty God, endue me with thy heavenly grace, that I may take up willingly any cross Thou puttest upon me, and with it follow after Thee. Of the cup Thou givest, though bitter to the taste, may I drink without murmuring against Thee. And in all my troubles, may I with unfeigned lips and heart say, the Lord giveth and taketh away ; blessed be the name of the Lord. *Amen.*

FOR GRACES.—Heavenly Father, let the blood of thy dear Son wash away the spots of my sins. Let His righteousness hide my unrighteousness. Let His deservings commend me to Thee. Let not my faith ,waver, nor my hope stagger, nor my love wax cold. Let me not be cast down by the fear of death ; but when death shall have closed the eyes of my body, let the eyes of my mind look still upon Thee. When it shall have bereft me of the use of my tongue, let my heart cry steadfastly unto Thee, " Into thy hands I commit my spirit, O Lord ;" to whom be honor and praise, world without end. *Amen.*

COMMENDATORY. — The Lord preserve my going out and my coming in, this day and for ever. *Amen.*

SATURDAY EVENING.

CONFESSION.—Almighty and most merciful Father, I confess at the close of this week, that I have sinned against heaven and in thy sight, and am not worthy to be called thy child. [Here make confession of special sins.] To Thee I come, who art the fountain of mercy. Unto Thee, whom I cannot endure as a judge, my soul crieth as unto a Saviour. To Thee, O Lord, I show my wounds ; to Thee I open my shame. My hope is in thy mercy. Pity me, full of misery and sin, O Thou, who art the fountain of pity. Save me by the life-giving sacrifice offered for me on the cross. Save me by that precious blood which washeth away the sins of the world. It grieveth me that I have sinned against Thee. Take from me all my sins. Purge them perfectly. Defend me now and evermore, by thine Almighty power, through the cross and intercession of thy Son, our Lord. *Amen.*

FOR PARDON.—O Thou, whose nature and property is ever to have mercy, receive my humble petitions ; and although I be tied and bound with the chain of my sins, yet let the pitifulness of thy great mercy loose me, for the honor and glory of Jesus Christ, our only Mediator and Advocate. *Amen.*

FOR GRACE.—Be not provoked, O Lord, by my many backslidings, to give me over to the devices and

desires of my own heart ; but strive Thou still with my
perverseness for Jesus' sake ; and let the precious
dews of thy grace distil upon and soften my hard
heart, and make it bring forth abundantly all thy
blessed fruits of love, joy, peace, long-suffering, gentleness, goodness, faith, meekness, temperance, and
charity ; through Jesus Christ, our Lord. *Amen.*

FOR BLESSINGS.—Grant, O God, that I may never
knowingly live one moment under thy displeasure. or
in any known sin.   Enable me to escape the corrup-
tion that is in the world through lust, and that I may
be a partaker of thy divine nature.   Keep me from
all things hurtful, and lead me to all things necessary
for my salvation.   Deliver me from every evil work,
and preserve me to thy heavenly kingdom.   Cleanse
me from all my sin, and help me to serve Thee with a
quiet and peaceful mind ; through Jesus Christ, our
Lord. *Amen.*

FOR OTHERS.—Let thy fatherly hand, O Lord, be
upon all whom Thou hast made.   Hear the prayers of
all who call upon Thee.   Open the eyes of them that
never pray for themselves.   Pity the sorrows of all
such as be in misery.   Preserve this land from the
evils of war, pestilence, and famine.   Keep thy Church
from all dangerous errors, and this people from forgetting Thee, the Lord their benefactor.   Bless all
persons to whom thy providence has made me a
debtor, and make me in turn useful to others.   Let
none that desire my prayers want thy mercy.   And

to God shall be all the glory, through Jesus Christ, our Lord. *Amen.*

FOR THE RIGHT USE OF THE LORD'S DAY.—Most gracious God, who hast given the night for the repose of our bodies, and holy seasons for the refreshment of our souls, teach me so to employ thy sacred day in thy worship and service, as to prepare me for that rest where all thy people shall, day and night, offer unto Thee sacrifices of praise and thanksgiving to the glory of thy holy name ; through Jesus Christ, our Lord. *Amen.*

AGAINST WORRIES.—O Lord Jesus Christ, who wast patient under provocation, and submissive under trial ; who didst warn thy people against the cares of life, bidding them take no anxious thought ; Thou knowest the anxieties, the cares, and the troubles I meet with. They be too heavy for me to bear ; but thou hast commanded us to cast them all upon Thee, because Thou carest for us. So I come to Thee, O loving Christ, and in humble confidence and meek submission would cast them upon Thee. O Christ, help me. Lord have mercy upon me. Christ have mercy upon me, and give me rest. *Amen* and *Amen.*

QUESTIONS FOR SELF-EXAMINATION.

I. Is there anything in my daily life I am afraid to look into?

II. Is there anything in my conduct I feel I could not justify in the eyes of persons I respect?

III. Is there anything I do now, which I intend some day to leave off doing?

IV. Am I honest in buying and selling, and in all my dealings with my fellow-men; and with the State in giving in all my taxable property?

V. Am I truthful and kind; pleasant and sincere in conversation; pure in thought and act?

VI. Am I sullen, pettish, impatient or passionate in temper?

VII. Am I in love and charity with my neighbors?

VIII. Do I devote a sufficient portion of my time and property to the support of the Gospel and the poor?

IX. Am I sorry for my sins? Do I daily confess them to God? Am I honestly striving and praying to be delivered from them?

X. Am I trusting for pardon only in the merits and atonement of the Lord Jesus Christ?

XI. Have I a good hope that I am pardoned? Am I striving for this as for other Christian graces?

XII. Am I ashamed of being known as a Christian? Do I honor my Christian profession? Do I bring disgrace upon the Christian church?

PRAYERS BEFORE HOLY COMMUNION.

O God, the searcher of hearts, prepare me to receive the Sacrament of Christ's Body and Blood with true piety and devotion. Pour thy grace into my soul, that I may go worthily to the sacred feast ; and of thy great goodness, give me what is wanting to help my weakness, and what is lacking to increase my faith ; through Jesus Christ. *Amen.*

Lord, I am invited to the communion of the most precious Body and Blood of thy dear Son. His mercy hath bestowed it, and my faith would receive it into my soul. Speak peace to my conscience, and enrich me with all graces, till I be possessed of eternal life in Christ. *Amen.*

Lord Jesus, I would draw nigh to thy table, to partake of Thee and all the benefits Thou hast purchased for me by thy precious blood-shedding. Help me to come with a penitent heart, in love and charity with my neighbors, with full purpose to lead a better life, keeping thy commandments, and walking in thy holy ways. May I draw near with faith ; may I take this holy Sacrament to my comfort, and be thereby refreshed in spirit, so that I may rejoice in Thee with all my heart. *Amen.*

O Lord, into a pure, charitable, thankful, and joyful heart, give me grace to receive the blessed Body and Blood of thy Son, my most blessed Saviour ; that He may more perfectly cleanse me from all my sins ; that being made clean, He may nourish me in faith, hope, charity, and obedience. Grant that in all the future course of my life, I may show myself such an ingrafted member of the body of thy Son, that I may never be drawn to do anything that may dishonor His name. Grant all this, for His merits, and mercy's sake. *Amen.*

Lord, though I be not worthy, yet am I invited to come and partake of Thyself. Lord, I come in obedience to Thee ; to eat and be thankful ; to drink and be refreshed. *Amen.*

Lord, I come to Thee in faith ; yet for the clearness of my faith, enlighten it ; for the strength of my faith, increase it ; and for the weakness of my love, enlarge it O Christ, give me thyself ; so that in Thee I may possess all good. *Amen.*

www.ingramcontent.com/pod-product-compliance
Lightning Source LLC
Chambersburg PA
CBHW031816090426
42739CB00008B/1296

* 9 7 8 3 3 3 7 2 8 4 9 6 1 *